GREAT MINDS® WIT & WISDOM

Grade 1 Module 2:
Creature Features

Student Edition

COPYRIGHT STATEMENT

Table of Contents

Name:

Handout 1A: The Ants & the Grasshopper

Directions: Follow along as the fable is read aloud.

One bright day in late autumn a family of Ants were bustling about in the warm sunshine, drying out the grain they had stored up during the summer, when a starving Grasshopper, his fiddle under his arm, came up and humbly begged for a bite to eat.

"What!" cried the Ants in surprise, "haven't you stored anything away for the winter? What in the world were you doing all last summer?"

"I didn't have time to store up any food," whined the Grasshopper; "I was so busy making music that before I knew it the summer was gone."

The Ants shrugged their shoulders in disgust.

"Making music, were you?" they cried. "Very well; now dance!" And they turned their backs on the Grasshopper and went on with their work.

Name:

Handout 1B: The Hare & the Tortoise

Directions: Follow along as the fable is read aloud.

A Hare was making fun of the Tortoise one day for being so slow.

"Do you ever get anywhere?" he asked with a mocking laugh.

"Yes," replied the Tortoise, "and I get there sooner than you think. I'll run you a race and prove it."

The Hare was much amused at the idea of running a race with the Tortoise, but for the fun of the thing he agreed. So the Fox, who had consented to act as judge, marked the distance and started the runners off.

The Hare was soon far out of sight, and to make the Tortoise feel very deeply how ridiculous it was for him to try a race with a Hare, he lay down beside the course to take a nap until the Tortoise should catch up.

The Tortoise meanwhile kept going slowly but steadily, and, after a time, passed the place where the Hare was sleeping. But the Hare slept on very peacefully; and when at last he did wake up, the Tortoise was near the goal. The Hare now ran his swiftest, but he could not overtake the Tortoise in time.

Name:

Handout 1C: Question Cubes

Directions: Cut out the shape below and fold on the dotted lines. Tape along the edges to form a cube. Roll the cube and form a question using the resulting word.

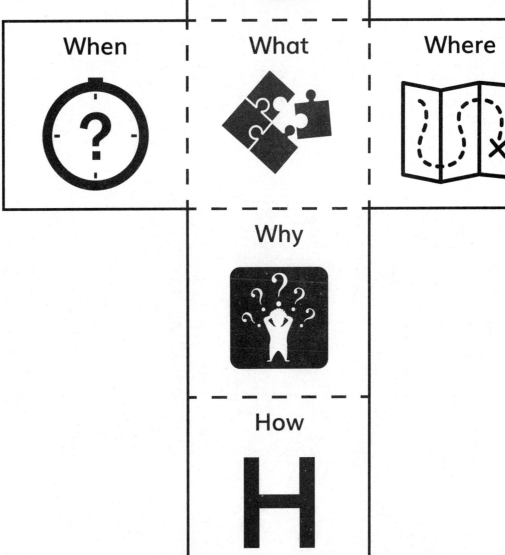

Name: _____

Handout 2A: Topic Sandwich Chart

Directions: Point to each component of the Topic Sandwich as you orally rehearse an informative paragraph.

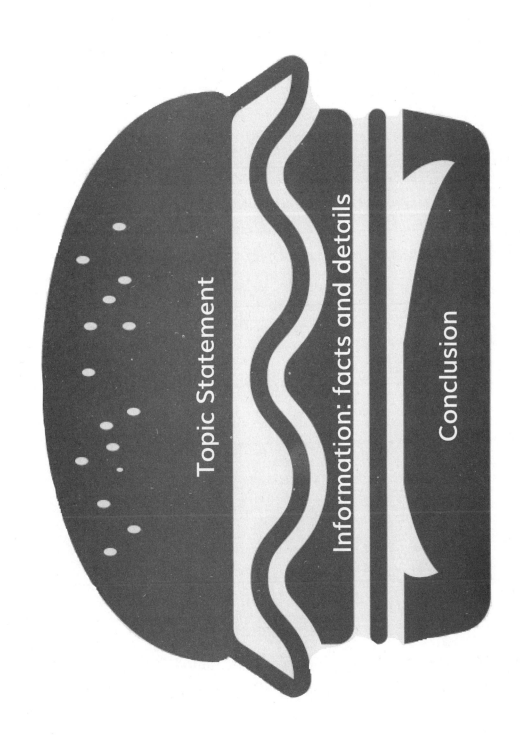

Topic Statement

Information: facts and details

Conclusion

Name:

Handout 2B: Fluency Homework

Directions: Read the text for homework. Have an adult or peer initial the unshaded boxes each day that you read the passage.

Option A

The Hare & the Tortoise, *Aesop's Fables*

The Tortoise kept going slowly but steadily. He passed the place where the Hare was sleeping.

The Hare now ran his fastest. He could not catch up to the Tortoise in time.

32 Words

Aesop. "The Hare & the Tortoise." *Library of Congress*. n.d. Web. 24 June 2016.

Student Performance Checklist:	Day 1		Day 2		Day 3	
	You	Listener*	You	Listener*	You	Listener*
Read the passage three to five times.						
Read with appropriate phrasing and pausing.						
Read with appropriate expression.						
Read at a good pace, not too fast and not too slow.						
Read to be heard and understood.						

*Adult or peer

Handout 2B: Fluency Homework

Directions: Read the text for homework. Have an adult or peer initial the unshaded boxes each day that you read the passage.

Option B

The Ants & the Grasshopper, *Aesop's Fables*

"What!" cried the Ants, "haven't you stored food away for the winter? What were you doing all last summer?"

"I didn't have time to store food," cried the Grasshopper; "I was busy making music. Before I knew it the summer was gone."

42 Words

Aesop. "The Ants & the Grasshopper." *Library of Congress*. n.d. Web. 24 June 2016.

Student Performance Checklist:	Day 1		Day 2		Day 3	
	You	Listener*	You	Listener*	You	Listener*
Read the passage three to five times.						
Read with appropriate phrasing and pausing.						
Read with appropriate expression.						
Read at a good pace, not too fast and not too slow.						
Read to be heard and understood.						

*Adult or peer

Name:

Handout 3A: Tortoises

Directions: Students annotate the components of an informative paragraph using colored pencils. Topic Statement = Light Green, Facts = Yellow, Conclusion = Dark Green

Tortoises

Tortoises are reptiles. Tortoises have large scales on their body. Tortoises have a shell. They lay eggs. Tortoises do not like cold weather. Tortoises are interesting reptiles.

Name:

Handout 3B: Movement Words

Directions: Cut apart the word cards.

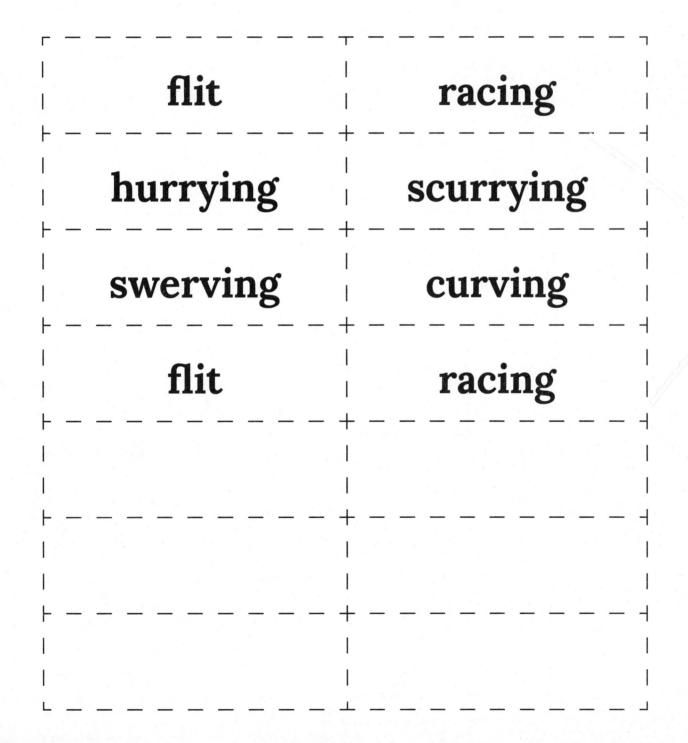

flit	racing
hurrying	scurrying
swerving	curving
flit	racing

Name:

Handout 4A: Punctuation Cards

Directions: Cut apart the punctuation cards.

Name:

Handout 5A: The Hare & the Tortoise Topic Sandwich

Directions: Write the details for the informative paragraph about "The Hare & the Tortoise."

The lesson of "The Hare & the Tortoise" is: even if you are slow, if you keep going you will win the race.

(Details)

The race is not always to the swift.

Name:

Handout 5B: Fluency Homework

Directions: Read the text for homework. Have an adult or peer initial the unshaded boxes each day that you read the passage.

Seven Blind Mice, Ed Young

Reader 1: Ah, now I see. The Something is

Reader 2: as sturdy as a pillar,

Reader 3: supple as a snake,

Reader 2: wide as a cliff,

Reader 3: sharp as a spear,

Reader 2: breezy as a fan,

Reader 3: stringy as a rope,

Reader 1: but altogether the Something is an elephant.

54 Words

Young, Ed. *Seven Blind Mice*. New York: Penguin Books, 1992.

Student Performance Checklist:	Day 1		Day 2		Day 3		Day 4		Day 5	
	You	Listener*	You	Listener*	You	Listener*	You	Listener*	You	Listener*
Read the passage three to five times.										
Read with appropriate phrasing and pausing.										
Read with appropriate expression.										
Read at a good pace, not too fast and not too slow.										
Read to be heard and understood.										

*Adult or peer

Name:

Handout 5C: Shades of Meaning Chart

Directions: Place the word cards from Handout 3B on the Shades of Meaning Chart from the slowest to the quickest movement.

move
to change positions or locations, to be in motion

Name: _____

Handout 6A: Informative Paragraph

Directions: Cut on the dotted lines. Glue the sentences in the correct order to create an informative paragraph.

Hares have strong back legs that help them run fast.

Helpful body parts help hares run and hear.

They have long ears and can hear other animals very well.

Hares have helpful body parts.

Name:

Topic Statement:

Details:

Conclusion:

Name: _____

Handout 7A: Elephant Parts

Directions: Draw the part of the elephant that the image represents from the text *Seven Blind Mice*.

Name:

Handout 7B: Elephant

Directions: Put drawings together to form an elephant.

Name:
_____

Handout 8A: Word Cards

Directions: Cut apart the word cards.

lesson	characteristics
message	advice
rules	end
fables	stories
kindness	wisdom

Name:

Handout 9A: Topic Sandwich Organizer

Directions: Use the Topic Sandwich to create your own informative paragraph.

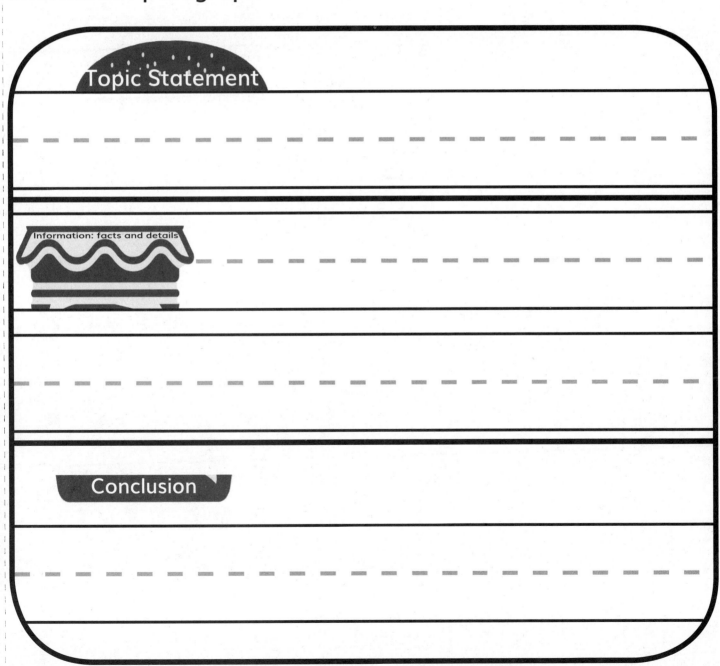

Name:

Handout 10A: Fluency Homework

Directions: Read the text for homework. Have an adult or peer initial the unshaded boxes each day that you read the passage.

Me...Jane, Patrick McDonnell

And Jane loved to be outside.
She watched birds making their nests,
spiders spinning their webs, and
squirrels chasing one another up and down trees.

27 Words

McDonnell, Patrick. *Me...Jane*. New York: Little, Brown and Company. 2011.

Student Performance Checklist:	Day 1		Day 2		Day 3		Day 4		Day 5	
	You	Listener*	You	Listener*	You	Listener*	You	Listener*	You	Listener*
Read the passage three to five times.										
Read with appropriate phrasing and pausing.										
Read with appropriate expression.										
Read at a good pace, not too fast and not too slow.										
Read to be heard and understood.										

*Adult or peer

Name:

Handout 11A: Buttons and Boxes

Directions: Cut on dotted lines. Say a detail and place a button in the box.

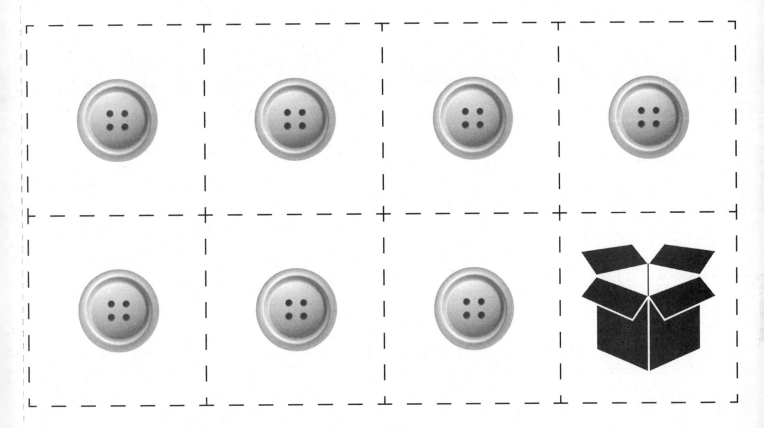

Name: _____

Handout 11B: Topic Statements

Directions: Determine the topic statement that best matches the paragraph. Color the box light green.

Jane wanted to play hide-and-seek.	Jane was curious about where eggs came from.

Jane and Jubilee went into her grandma's chicken coop.
They hid behind some straw.
They stayed very still.
Jane and Jubilee saw the chicken lay the egg.

Directions: Write a topic statement for the paragraph below in the space provided.

Topic Statement:

_____

- -

_____

- -

_____

- -

_____

Jane watched birds making their nests.
She watched spiders spinning their webs.
She watched squirrels chase each other.
Jane learned all that she could about animals.

Name:

Handout 11C: Shades of Meaning Chart

Directions: Write the words from the class list.

observe

Name: _____

Handout 12A: Shades of Meaning Chart

Directions: Write the words from the class list.

cherish

Name:

Handout 15A: Fluency Homework

Directions: Read the text for homework. Have an adult or peer initial the unshaded boxes each day that you read the passage.

Sea Horse: The Shyest Fish in the Sea, Chris Butterworth

Sea Horse has a head like a horse,
a tail like a monkey,
and a pouch like a kangaroo.
Sea Horse swims upright.
He moves himself through the water
with the little fins on his head and
the larger one on his back.

43 Words

Butterworth, Chris. *Sea Horse: The Shyest Fish in the Sea*. Massachusetts: Candlewick Press, 2006.

Student Performance Checklist:	Day 1		Day 2		Day 3		Day 4		Day 5		Day 6	
	You	Listener*	You	Listener*	You	Listener*	You	Listener*	You	Listener*	You	Listener*
Read the passage three to five times.												
Read with appropriate phrasing and pausing.												
Read with appropriate expression.												
Read at a good pace, not too fast and not too slow.												
Read to be heard and understood.												

*Adult or peer

Name: _____

Handout 18A: Sea Horse Details

Directions: Circle two details to include in your informative paragraph.

Tail	Pouch
Twists tails together with mate	Female puts eggs in the male's pouch
Uncurls tail to rise up in the water	Male seals the pouch
Curls tail to drop down in the water	Male gives birth to the babies
Tail can hold on to things	**Eye**
	Eye is like a black bead
	One eye looks up and one eye looks down
	Can see food from any direction

Name:

Handout 21A: Fluency Homework

Directions: Read the text for homework. Have an adult or peer initial the unshaded boxes each day that you read the passage.

Option A

What Do You Do With a Tail Like This? Steve Jenkins

What do you do with ears like these?
If you're a jackrabbit, you use your ears to keep cool.
If you're a cricket, you hear with ears that are on your knees.
If you're a bat, you "see" with your ears.
Animals uses their noses, ears, tails, eyes, mouths, and feet in very different ways.

41 Words

Jenkins, Steve. *What Do You Do With a Tail Like This?* Houghton Mifflin Company, 2003.

Student Performance Checklist:	Day 1		Day 2		Day 3		Day 4		Day 5	
	You	Listener*	You	Listener*	You	Listener*	You	Listener*	You	Listener*
Read the passage three to five times.										
Read with appropriate phrasing and pausing.										
Read with appropriate expression.										
Read at a good pace, not too fast and not too slow.										
Read to be heard and understood.										

*Adult or peer

Handout 21A: Fluency Homework

Directions: Read the text for homework. Have an adult or peer initial the unshaded boxes each day that you read the passage.

Option B

What Do You Do With a Tail Like This? Steve Jenkins

What do you do with a tail like this?
If you're a lizard, you break off your tail to get away.
If you're a skunk, you lift your tail to warn that a stinky spray is on the way.
If you're a monkey, you hang from a tree by your tail.
Animals uses their noses, ears, tails, eyes, mouths, and feet in very different ways.

51 Words

Jenkins, Steve. *What Do You Do With a Tail Like This?* Houghton Mifflin Company, 2003.

Student Performance Checklist:	Day 1		Day 2		Day 3		Day 4		Day 5	
	You	Listener*	You	Listener*	You	Listener*	You	Listener*	You	Listener*
Read the passage three to five times.										
Read with appropriate phrasing and pausing.										
Read with appropriate expression.										
Read at a good pace, not too fast and not too slow.										
Read to be heard and understood.										

*Adult or peer

Name:

Handout 27A: Fluency Homework

Directions: Read the text for homework. Have an adult or peer initial the unshaded boxes each day that you read the passage.

Never Smile at a Monkey, Steve Jenkins

NEVER collect a cone shell.
NEVER step on a stingray.
NEVER poach a puffer fish.
NEVER cuddle a cub.
NEVER stare at a spitting cobra.
NEVER touch a tang.
NEVER swim with a squid.
NEVER smile at a monkey!

39 Words

Jenkins, Steve. *Never Smile at a Monkey*. Houghton Mifflin Harcourt, 2003.

Student Performance Checklist:	Day 1		Day 2		Day 3		Day 4		Day 5		Day 6	
	You	Listener*	You	Listener*	You	Listener*	You	Listener*	You	Listener*	You	Listener*
Read the passage three to five times.												
Read with appropriate phrasing and pausing.												
Read with appropriate expression.												
Read at a good pace, not too fast and not too slow.												
Read to be heard and understood.												

*Adult or peer

Name:

Handout 27B: Sentence Frame

Directions: Finish the sentence and draw a picture to illustrate it.

Two attributes of _____ are _____ and _____.

Name:

Handout 29A: Write a Conclusion

Directions: Listen carefully as your teacher reads the paragraph. Write a conclusion for the paragraph in the space provided below.

The Electric Caterpillar is a colorful caterpillar that some people may want to touch.

The hairy bristles on the caterpillar will stick in your skin and burn. If you don't go to the doctor, you could get sick and even die.

Conclusion:

Name:

Handout 29B: Sentence Frame

Directions: Finish the sentence with a prepositional phrase and draw a picture to illustrate it.

I found my toy (in/by) _____ .

Name:

Handout 32A: Informative Writing Checklist

Directions: Circle the happy face if you included the component of an informative paragraph or a calm face if you did not include the component and need more practice.

Grade 1 Informative Writing Checklist			
	Self	Peer	Teacher
Structure			
I have a topic statement that names my topic.	😐 😊	😐 😊	😐 😊
I have 2 or more facts or details to support my topic statement.	😐 😊	😐 😊	😐 😊
I have a conclusion.	😐 😊	😐 😊	😐 😊
Conventions			
I used complete sentences.	😐 😊	😐 😊	😐 😊
I used end punctuation. . ? !	😐 😊	😐 😊	😐 😊
I used my best spelling.	😐 😊	😐 😊	😐 😊

Name: _____

Handout 32B: Word Cards

Directions: Cut apart the word cards.

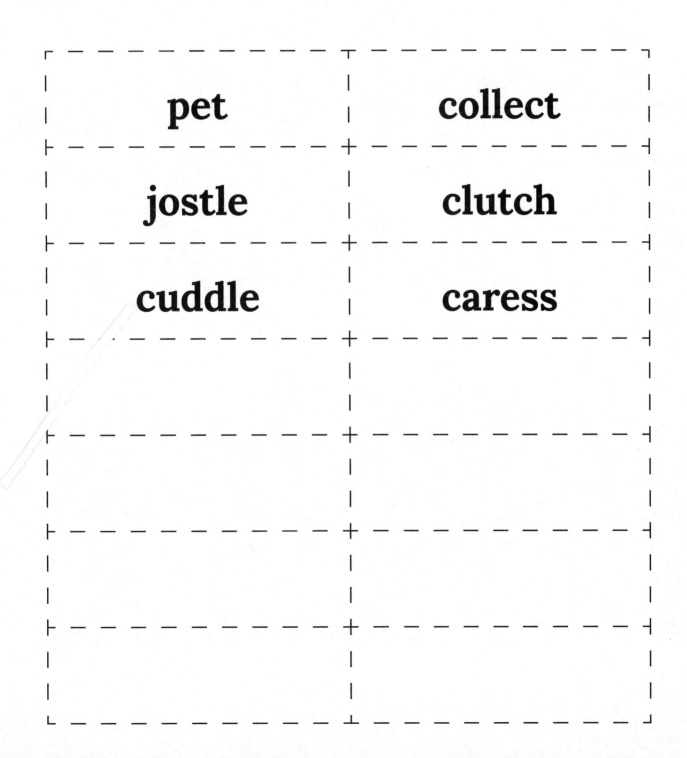

pet	collect
jostle	clutch
cuddle	caress

Name:

Handout 32C: Shades of Meaning Chart

Directions: Place the words from the text on the chart.

touch

Name: _____

Handout 33A: Animal Evidence Organizer

Directions: Select an animal. Then circle two details that tell about the animal's unique features.

- -

Hippopotamus

What is unique about this animal's features?

- -

- Ears have hair in them

- -

- Large gray body

- -

- Closes ears when it goes under water

- -

- Skin is easily sunburned

- -

- Has enormous mouth and long tusks that it uses to attack

- -

- Has sensitive skin

- -

Name:

Platypus

What is unique about this animal's features?

- Flat, wide, gray nose

- Brown body

- Uses its bill to dig through the mud for food

- Feet are webbed

- Males have poisonous spurs on their back legs

- Can use its bill to notice electric pulses from its prey

- The poisonous spur won't cause humans to die, but some people can be in a lot of pain for weeks

Name:

Chimpanzee

What is unique about this animal's features?

- Brown furry arm

- Hands don't have fur

- Hands have five fingers

- Feeds itself with its feet

- Has an opposable thumb, like humans

- Feet can grasp objects like a hand

- Has an opposable big toe that allows them to pick up and manipulate things with their feet

Name:

Handout 36A: Socratic Seminar Self-Assessment

A = I always did that.
S = I sometimes did that.
N = I'll do that next time.

Directions: Rate your participation.

Expectation	Evaluation (A, S, N)
I followed our class rules for the seminar.	
I responded to what others said at least once.	
I spoke in complete sentences.	
I noticed pauses.	
I readied my body to listen.	
I listened with my whole body.	

Volume of Reading Reflection Questions

Creature Features, Grade 1, Module 2

Student Name:

Text:

Author:

Topic:

Genre/type of book:

Share what you know about different creature features by sharing the answers to the question. Draw, write, or tell your teacher your answers.

Informational Texts

1. **Wonder:** What do you wonder when you look at the title and illustrations on the cover of this book?

2. **Organize:** What kinds of information does the author tell you about the animals described in this book?

3. **Reveal:** How does the author or illustrator show different features of animals? Find one place in the text that shows an interesting feature. How is that feature helpful to the animal?

4. **Distill:** What is the most important idea about creature features that you learned by reading this text? Draw a picture showing this idea and explain your drawing on the paper or to your teacher.

5. **Know:** What new information do you now know about animal features? Share three new things you learned.

6. **Vocabulary:** What are three important vocabulary words that you learned when reading this book? Why are they important words to know? Create a drawing and a sentence that explains one of the words you chose.

Literary Texts

1. **Wonder:** What do you wonder about the story, based on the title and illustrations on the cover?

2. **Organize:** What happened in this story? Draw a picture of your favorite part of the story.

3. **Reveal:** How does the author use illustrations to tell us more of the story? Show one illustration and explain how you learned more story details from looking closely.

4. **Distill:** Did any of the characters in this story learn a lesson? What lesson did they learn?

5. **Know:** How are imaginary animals different from real animals in stories? How are they like real animals in stories?

6. **Vocabulary:** What are three important vocabulary words that you learned when reading this book? Why are they important words to know? Create a drawing and a sentence that explains one of the words you chose.

WIT & WISDOM PARENT TIP SHEET

WHAT IS MY FIRST-GRADE STUDENT LEARNING IN MODULE 2?

Wit & Wisdom is our English curriculum. It builds knowledge of key topics in history, science, and literature through the study of excellent texts. By reading and responding to stories and nonfiction texts, we will build knowledge of the following topics:

Module 1: A World of Books

Module 2: Creature Features

Module 3: Powerful Forces

Module 4: Cinderella Stories

In Module 2, *Creature Features*, we will study the unique features of animals. We will ask: *What makes animals so fascinating? How do we observe, learn about, and engage with animals? How are the features of animals' bodies and behavior similar to and different from one another?*

OUR CLASS WILL READ THESE BOOKS:

Picture Books (Informational)

- *Me...Jane*, Patrick McDonnell
- *Never Smile at a Monkey*, Steve Jenkins
- *Sea Horse: The Shyest Fish in the Sea*, Chris Butterworth, John Lawrence
- *What Do You Do With a Tail Like This?*, Steve Jenkins, Robin Page

Picture Books (Literary)

- *Seven Blind Mice*, Ed Young

Fables

- "The Hare & the Tortoise," *Aesop's Fables*
- "The Ants & the Grasshopper," *Aesop's Fables*

OUR CLASS WILL WATCH THIS VIDEO:

- "Pygmy Sea Horses: Masters of Camouflage," Deep Look (2014)

OUR CLASS WILL EXAMINE THESE PAINTINGS:

- *Young Hare*, Albrecht Dürer (1502)
- *The Snail*, Henri Matisse (1953)

OUR CLASS WILL ASK THESE QUESTIONS:

- What lessons can we learn through stories about animals?
- How did Jane Goodall make discoveries about animals?
- How do sea horses use their unique features?
- How do animals use the same feature in unique ways?
- How do animals use their unique features in unexpected ways?
- What can we discover about animals' unique features?

QUESTIONS TO ASK AT HOME:

As you read with your first-grade student, ask:

- *What's happening?*
- *What does a closer look at words and illustrations reveal about this text's deeper meaning?*

BOOKS TO READ AT HOME:

- *Creature Features*, Steve Jenkins and Robin Page
- *Sisters and Brothers*, Steve Jenkins and Robin Page
- *How to Clean a Hippopotamus*, Steve Jenkins and Robin Page
- *My First Day*, Steve Jenkins and Robin Page
- *Where in the Wild?*, David Schwartz and Yael Schy
- *Where Else in the Wild?*, David Schwartz and Yael Schy
- *Unusual Creatures: A Mostly Accurate Account of the Earth's Strangest Animals*, Michael Hearst
- *Fur, Fins, and Feathers: Abraham Dee Bartlett and the Invention of the Modern Zoo*, Cassandre Maxwell
- *Starfish*, Edith Thacher Hurd
- *Sharks*, Kate Riggs
- *Amazing Animals: Dolphins*, Kate Riggs
- *Gentle Giant Octopus*, Karen Wallace
- *Surprising Sharks*, Nicola Davies

- *Giant Squid: Mystery of the Deep*, Jennifer Dussling
- *Big Blue Whale*, Nicola Davies
- *Amazing Animals: Cheetah*, Kate Riggs
- *Amazing Animals: Elephants*, Kate Riggs
- *Walk with a Wolf*, Janni Howker
- *Biggest, Strongest, Fastest*, Steve Jenkins
- *A Tower of Giraffes*, Anna Wright
- *The Happy Lion*, Louise Fatio
- *Unlovable*, Dan Yaccarino
- *Inch by Inch*, Leo Lionni
- *Amazing Animals: Eagles*, Kate Riggs
- *Bat Loves the Night*, Nicola Davies
- *Grasshopper on the Road*, Arnold Lobel
- *Behold the Beautiful Dung Beetle*, Cheryl Bardoe
- *Yucky Worms*, Vivian French
- *Chameleons Are Cool*, Martin Jenkins
- *The Beetle Book*, Steve Jenkins
- *The Iridescence of Birds: A Book about Henri Matisse*, Patricia MacLachlan
- *The Circus Ship*, Chris Van Dusen
- *Henri's Scissors*, Jeanette Winter
- *The Cat and the Bird: Children's Book Inspired by Paul Klee*, Géraldine Elschner
- *A Bird or Two: A Story About Henri Matisse*, Bijou le Tord
- *The Lives of the Artists: Masterpieces, Messes (and What the Neighbors Thought)*, Kathleen Krull

PLACES YOU CAN VISIT TO TALK ABOUT ANIMALS:

Visit a zoo, farm, or pet shop together. Ask:

- *What do you notice and wonder about the animals?*
- *What are some of the unique features of this animal?*
- *How does this animal use these unique features?*

You could ask these same questions at home about a family pet.

CREDITS

Great Minds® has made every effort to obtain permission for the reprinting of all copyrighted material. If any owner of copyrighted material is not acknowledged herein, please contact Great Minds® for proper acknowledgment in all future editions and reprints of this module.

- All material from the *Common Core State Standards for English Language Arts & Literacy in History/Social Studies, Science, and Technical Subjects* © Copyright 2010 National Governors Association Center for Best Practices and Council of Chief State School Officers. All rights reserved.

- The Painted Essay® is used by permission of Diana Leddy.

- All images are used under license from Shutterstock.com unless otherwise noted.

- For updated credit information, please visit http://witeng.link/credits.

ACKNOWLEDGMENTS

Great Minds® Staff

The following writers, editors, reviewers, and support staff contributed to the development of this curriculum.

Ann Brigham, Lauren Chapalee, Sara Clarke, Emily Climer, Lorraine Griffith, Emily Gula, Sarah Henchey, Trish Huerster, Stephanie Kane-Mainier, Lior Klirs, Liz Manolis, Andrea Minich, Lynne Munson, Marya Myers, Rachel Rooney, Aaron Schifrin, Danielle Shylit, Rachel Stack, Sarah Turnage, Michelle Warner, Amy Wierzbicki, Margaret Wilson, and Sarah Woodard.

Colleagues and Contributors

We are grateful for the many educators, writers, and subject-matter experts who made this program possible.

David Abel, Robin Agurkis, Elizabeth Bailey, Julianne Barto, Amy Benjamin, Andrew Biemiller, Charlotte Boucher, Sheila Byrd-Carmichael, Eric Carey, Jessica Carloni, Janine Cody, Rebecca Cohen, Elaine Collins, Tequila Cornelious, Beverly Davis, Matt Davis, Thomas Easterling, Jeanette Edelstein, Kristy Ellis, Moira Clarkin Evans, Charles Fischer, Marty Gephart, Kath Gibbs, Natalie Goldstein, Christina Gonzalez, Mamie Goodson, Nora Graham, Lindsay Griffith, Brenna Haffner, Joanna Hawkins, Elizabeth Haydel, Steve Hettleman, Cara Hoppe, Ashley Hymel, Carol Jago, Jennifer Johnson, Mason Judy, Gail Kearns, Shelly Knupp, Sarah Kushner, Shannon Last, Suzanne Lauchaire, Diana Leddy, David Liben, Farren Liben, Jennifer Marin, Susannah Maynard, Cathy McGath, Emily McKean, Jane Miller, Rebecca Moore, Cathy Newton, Turi Nilsson, Julie Norris, Galemarie Ola, Michelle Palmieri, Meredith Phillips, Shilpa Raman, Tonya Romayne, Emmet Rosenfeld, Jennifer Ruppel, Mike Russoniello, Deborah Samley, Casey Schultz, Renee Simpson, Rebecca Sklepovich, Amelia Swabb, Kim Taylor, Vicki Taylor, Melissa Thomson, Lindsay Tomlinson, Melissa Vail, Keenan Walsh, Julia Wasson, Lynn Welch, Yvonne Guerrero Welch, Emily Whyte, Lynn Woods, and Rachel Zindler.

Early Adopters

The following early adopters provided invaluable insight and guidance for Wit & Wisdom:

- Bourbonnais School District 53 • Bourbonnais, IL
- Coney Island Prep Middle School • Brooklyn, NY
- Gate City Charter School for the Arts • Merrimack, NH
- Hebrew Academy for Special Children • Brooklyn, NY
- Paris Independent Schools • Paris, KY
- Saydel Community School District • Saydel, IA
- Strive Collegiate Academy • Nashville, TN
- Valiente College Preparatory Charter School • South Gate, CA
- Voyageur Academy • Detroit, MI

Design Direction provided by Alton Creative, Inc.

Project management support, production design, and copyediting services provided by ScribeConcepts.com

Copyediting services provided by Fine Lines Editing

Product management support provided by Sandhill Consulting